B   Franchere, Ruth
Cha
           Cesar Chavez

CESAR CHAVEZ

Thomas Y. Crowell • New York

CESAR CHAVEZ

By Ruth Franchere

Illustrated by Earl Thollander

CROWELL BIOGRAPHIES
Edited by Susan Bartlett Weber

JANE ADDAMS *by Gail Faithfull Keller*

MARIAN ANDERSON *by Tobi Tobias*

LEONARD BERNSTEIN *by Molly Cone*

MARTHA BERRY *by Mary Kay Phelan*

WILT CHAMBERLAIN *by Kenneth Rudeen*

RAY CHARLES *by Sharon Bell Mathis*

CESAR CHAVEZ *by Ruth Franchere*

SAMUEL CLEMENS
by Charles Michael Daugherty

ROBERTO CLEMENTE *by Kenneth Rudeen*

CHARLES DREW *by Roland Bertol*

FANNIE LOU HAMER *by June Jordan*

LANGSTON HUGHES, AMERICAN POET
by Alice Walker

JAMES WELDON JOHNSON
by Ophelia Settle Egypt

FIORELLO LA GUARDIA
by Mervyn Kaufman

THE MAYO BROTHERS *by Jane Goodsell*

JOHN MUIR *by Charles P. Graves*

JESSE OWENS *by Mervyn Kaufman*

GORDON PARKS *by Midge Turk*

ROSA PARKS *by Eloise Greenfield*

THE RINGLING BROTHERS *by Molly Cone*

JACKIE ROBINSON *by Kenneth Rudeen*

ELEANOR ROOSEVELT *by Jane Goodsell*

MARIA TALLCHIEF *by Tobi Tobias*

JIM THORPE *by Thomas Fall*

THE WRIGHT BROTHERS
by Ruth Franchere

MALCOLM X *by Arnold Adoff*

Published in Canada by Fitzhenry & Whiteside Limited, Toronto.

Manufactured in the United States of America

L.C. Card 78—101927

ISBN 0-690-18383-6
ISBN 0-690-18384-4 (LB)

5 6 7 8 9 10

CESAR CHAVEZ

Blistering sun beats down on the dry, desert land near Yuma, Arizona. Tall cactus plants called prickly pear and Joshua trees stand like silent men upon the sandy ground.

I

Here on a little farm Cesar Chavez once lived
with his parents and five brothers and sisters.

2

Until he was ten years old, he felt the scorching earth under his bare feet. He knew the sting of hot dust on his brown skin.

Cesar's grandfather had come to the United States from Mexico. With other Mexicans he had settled on free land in Arizona.

Grandfather had cut down cactus and plowed and watered the sandy soil of his little farm. He had planted melons, peppers, corn, and beans. He worked very hard.

Later, Cesar's parents worked on the same farm from dawn until dark. The older children helped them. At first Cesar stayed at home with the other small children. But as soon as he was old enough he helped, too. He pulled weeds and carried water.

Cesar's family grew the food for their meals. If they had any extra vegetables, they took them to Yuma and sold them. With the money they received, they bought a few clothes. But some of the children had to go barefoot, even in winter. No one had good clothes to wear to church on Sundays.

Cesar's family all had dark skin and dark hair. They spoke only Spanish. Even though they were born in the United States, they were called Mexican-Americans.

During the years when he was very young, Cesar often heard his father and mother say that the United States was having hard times. Many people were poor. In Yuma some did not even have the money to buy vegetables.

In 1937, when Cesar was ten years old, his parents told him that they would not be able to stay on the farm any longer. They explained that all the farmers had to pay money, called taxes, to the state of Arizona. If they could not pay, they had to give their farms back to the state.

The Chavez family did not earn enough money that year for the taxes. Neither did their neighbors. They all went to their Catholic priest for advice. They thought he could help because he could speak English and they could not.

The priest wanted very much to help his people. Sadly, he repeated that the taxes had to be

paid or they must leave. He was sorry that he did
not have the money to give them.

9

For a while, all the people were worried and
frightened. They did not know what to do.

10

Then men called labor contractors came to Yuma. They came to find workers for large farms in California. They told the poor farmers that they could earn a great deal of money as migrant workers going from one farm to another to pick cotton, vegetables, and fruit.

Cesar's father and mother talked about what they had heard. They knew there was no work for them in Yuma. They decided to go to California.

One hot day they rolled up their old bedding and roped some buckets and pans together. They wrapped up a few keepsakes. Mrs. Chavez carefully packed the beautiful lace that she had made. Then they tied the bundles on top of their old Studebaker.

The parents and six children got into the car and rode west toward the bridge over the Colorado River, just a few miles away. They knew that when they crossed the river they would be in the Imperial Valley of California. There the farms would be very large and green.

Ahead of them, and behind them, were other old cars loaded with bundles and children. All were heading for the land where they had been told they would have a better life.

The Chavez family were sad to leave their home, but they were excited, too. Cesar's parents believed they could earn enough money so their children would not have to work. They could go to school and learn to read and write and speak English.

Cesar did not take up much room in the old car. He was small and thin. But he was sure he

could work and earn money. Maybe he could buy some shoes and a new shirt. His old shirt was almost worn out. His brother Richard needed shoes, too. Maybe they could work together.

Finally they reached a large farm where a labor contractor had told them they would find jobs. They looked around for a place to live, but saw only some old, one-room shacks made out of sheet metal. Those couldn't be places for people to live in, they thought.

They looked at one. It was as hot as an oven inside. There was no running water, no bathroom, and only one gas burner to cook on.

Tired and discouraged, they went back to the car and wondered what to do. Other families drove up and began to move into the shacks.

At last Mr. Chavez untied the bedding from the Studebaker. Mrs. Chavez carried her pots and pans into the one room. Cesar got a bucket. He filled it from a faucet in the yard and carried the water to his mother.

As the sun went down, the family ate a cold supper. Then they spread the bedding on the floor of the hot shack. Fearful and homesick, they lay down and tried to sleep.

That was the beginning of Cesar's life among the migrant workers. As time went on, life for all the workers became worse instead of better. Most of the work was called "stoop labor." The pickers

had to bend over all day long. Their backs ached and they were always very tired.

They stayed at a farm until the crop of vegetables or fruit or cotton was picked. Their final pay was often much less than they had been promised. But because they could not speak English they could not argue.

They took what they were given and moved to wherever the labor contractors sent them. They traveled north to the San Joaquin Valley of central California and back again—wherever there were crops to pick.

Sometimes the crops were very poor and the workers did not earn enough to buy food. They could not buy gasoline for their cars. Sometimes there were no shacks so they slept in their cars or in tents.

All one rainy winter Cesar's family camped under a bridge. Another time, when the picking was finished, they had no money even for gasoline. They wrote to some relatives in Arizona for help. After all the other workers left the camp, the owner turned off the electricity. Then they waited in a dark shack, frightened and hungry, for several days. Finally they received enough money from Arizona to get them to Los Angeles.

There Mrs. Chavez asked her husband to stop the car. She unwrapped the lace she had crocheted on the farm near Yuma. Then she got out and walked along the street selling it. With the money she earned they bought a little food and enough gasoline to get to another farm.

In winter there was very little work for the pickers. During those months Mr. and Mrs. Chavez tried to stay in one place so their children could go to school. They did any sort of work for a little food. But often they could stay only a few days or weeks before the work ran out and they had to move on.

By the time Cesar had finished the eighth grade, he had gone to about three dozen schools. He sat at his desk and listened and learned some English. But the teachers did not pay much attention to the migrant pupils who spoke Spanish

among themselves. They knew the ragged children would move away soon and many more would take their places.

When Cesar knew the answer to a question, he wanted to raise his hand and recite. But he was too shy. He was afraid the others would laugh at him.

After school, Cesar and Richard fished in the canals that brought water from rivers to the fields. They hunted wild mustard greens for their mother to cook for supper. They were always hungry.

From along the roads they collected old ciga-
rette packages and gum wrappers that were lined
with tinfoil. They smoothed out the tinfoil and
formed it into a ball. When the ball weighed
eighteen pounds, they sold it for a few dollars and
bought tennis shoes and two shirts. That was an
exciting day. On weekends and vacations they
worked in the fields with their parents.

22

In the valleys of California, people with light skins who are not Mexican are called "Anglos." Cesar talked to Anglo field workers in English. From them he learned many things about the different farms and owners. He found out on which farms he could make the most money and where he would not be cheated. He learned where the housing was poor.

Cesar explained these things to his parents. He told other Mexican-American families and new workers from Mexico, too. He did not want them to suffer as he and his family had.

Finally, the family grew tired of moving. They settled in a tumbledown shack near San Jose, California, not far from some large farms. There they could usually find work. As soon as Cesar was old enough, he left his family and found a job on his own.

Cesar preferred to work in the vineyards. He liked to walk down the long rows of grapevines and see the new leaves sprout in the spring. He watched the bunches of grapes swell and ripen in the sun during the summer.

In some ways it was miserable work. Under the vines, where the great bunches of grapes hung, gnats swarmed over his arms and face. The air was stifling. His back ached from the long hours of stoop labor.

But in the vineyards, some work went on most of the year. He did not have to migrate from one job to another. He slept in barracks and had regular meals with other men. Best of all, he became skilled in handling the grapes and pruning and training the vines. He took pride in doing work that a beginner could not do.

Cesar could not forget his childhood, however. The families with many children still lived in crowded, filthy shacks.

He talked with other workers about going to the owners and asking for better houses and more pay. But most of the workers were afraid they would lose their jobs. They had families to feed.

At about that time, in Delano, California, Cesar met a girl named Helen Fabela. She believed in what he was trying to do for the workers. He fell in love with her and wanted to marry her.

But World War II had begun, so first Cesar joined the Navy. He was proud to serve his country.

One day when he was on leave, he returned to Delano to see Helen. He took her to a movie. After they sat down, an usher told them they were in the section reserved for Anglos. He asked Cesar to move across the aisle where the Mexican-Americans were supposed to sit.

Cesar was not a violent person. He usually spoke in a kind, soft voice. But he was very angry.

He protested. He refused to move. He was a Navy man, an American.

At last he and Helen were told to get out.

Cesar strode up the aisle beside Helen. At once he made up his mind. As soon as the war was over, he would work day and night to get respect and justice for his people.

After the war ended, Cesar married Helen. He worked for a while near San Jose picking apricots for only sixty-five cents an hour.

Cesar tried to get fellow workers to join him in demanding better pay. But most of them were still afraid of the farm owners. The Mexicans who were not citizens were sure they would be sent home if they complained. In Mexico, life was even harder than in California.

So Cesar organized classes where Mexicans could learn to read and write English. He wanted them to be able to pass the tests to become United States citizens. Then they would not be so afraid.

One day an Anglo named Fred Ross came to San Jose. He heard what Cesar was doing and wanted to talk to him. But Cesar had been cheated and mistreated by Anglos. He did not trust them. For a long time he refused to see Fred Ross.

When at last they met, Cesar was surprised that Ross wanted to help the workers. He talked about the things that Cesar believed in. He explained that he was an organizer for the Community Service Organization.

Cesar was excited. When Fred Ross asked him to work for the organization, he agreed to at once.

Cesar picked apricots in the daytime. In the evenings he called on Mexican-Americans who were United States citizens. He worked hard to persuade them to register so they could vote like other Americans. In two months he registered more than four thousand workers.

Soon the farm owners learned what he was doing. Because they all feared that he would stir up trouble among the workers, Cesar's boss fired him.

Then Cesar took a full-time job with the Community Service Organization. He made $325 a month. That was more than he had ever earned in his life. But the money was not important. His work was all that interested him.

One of Cesar's jobs was to organize meetings. He worried all the time because he did not know how to lead a meeting. He had never learned to express himself well. So he studied in every spare minute. He listened carefully to other speakers.

Gradually he found that workers would listen to him and accept what he said. They liked him because he listened to them and understood their problems.

One by one, Cesar persuaded people to join the organization. It was very hard work. The workers were always afraid they, too, would be fired. Getting the Mexican workers to go to citizenship classes was difficult, too. They would promise to go and then stay at home. Sometimes he had to be tough and call them cowards.

Cesar grew impatient. In March 1962, when he was thirty-five years old, he decided to leave the Community Service Organization. He and Helen had small children now. They moved back to flat, dusty Delano and rented a little, old house. It was on the west side of town where other Mexican-Americans lived. The Anglos lived on the east side.

Cesar and Helen had saved twelve hundred dollars. With it they planned to organize and help farm workers in the San Joaquin Valley around Delano. To earn a living for their own family, Helen went to work in the fields. Sometimes Cesar dug ditches on Sundays.

They called their new organization the National Farm Workers Association or NFWA.

For six months Cesar traveled from one camp

of migrants to another. He found a few eager workers in each camp who got others to join the NFWA.

When he had signed up three hundred members, he decided to have a meeting. He and his cousin, Manuel, designed a flag. It was red, with a black eagle in a white circle in the center. He showed it to the members at the first meeting. They liked it very much.

Then Cesar explained that, if each family paid a small amount, the NFWA would help them. It would start grocery stores and drugstores and filling stations where they could buy things cheap. It would hire lawyers to help those who might be cheated because they could not read English. It would even lend them money.

When the three hundred members heard Cesar's plans, they clapped and cheered. After the meeting they got many more members for the NFWA.

During the next three years, Cesar did all the things he had promised. At the same time, he was making even more important plans.

He knew there were laws to protect workers in stores and factories. They had to be paid fair wages and have clean working conditions.

But there were no such laws for farm workers. Growers could pay them as little as they liked. They could make them work for long hours every day without any rest periods. They did not have to give them clean places in which to live.

Cesar was determined to change all this. As soon as the association was large enough, he wanted the members to demand the same rights for themselves that other workers had.

But in 1965, some grape pickers who were not NFWA members became impatient. They needed to earn more money during the harvest season. In the winter, they knew, there would be no work.

34

At several vineyards they demanded $1.40 an hour and 25 cents for each box of grapes they picked.

They threatened: "We will stop working! We will strike! Your grapes will rot on the vines!"

But the vineyard owners refused to raise the pay. So those pickers lined up at the edge of the fields. They shouted "Strike!" or the Spanish word for strike, *"Huelga!"* They wanted all the other pickers to leave the fields and join them.

35

Cesar was not ready for a big strike. He had only $87. He worried about the many people who would need food during a strike. But his followers urged him to join. At last he agreed. Then the NFWA members stood near the fields and shouted "Strike!" or "*Huelga!*" too.

For many weeks, owners and strikers argued and fought. But at last the owners of two vineyards agreed to raise wages. Strikers there went back to work.

Then another strike began at one of the largest vineyards. This time the workers demanded that Cesar Chavez be allowed to speak for all of them. The owner refused. Instead, he brought in truckloads of workers from Mexico.

The Mexicans did not know about the trouble. They could not understand English. When they heard "*huelga*" they did not know what it meant. So the strike went on and on.

By this time Cesar had become famous. Stories about him were in newspapers and magazines all over the country.

Many people who read the stories believed in what Cesar was doing. Priests, ministers, rabbis, nuns, students, and others went to Delano to help him. They answered letters, worked in the stores, and carried meals and cool drinks to the strikers. Other people sent food, clothing, and money.

Cesar was very grateful. But still the strike went on. Delano became more bitter and divided every day. Cesar could see no way of ending the strike there.

One day he had a new idea. If so many people all over the country sympathized with the farm workers, perhaps they could help in a different way. Maybe they would agree not to buy any grapes—to boycott them—until the growers would bargain with the workers.

Cesar called a meeting of the strikers. He told them about his new idea. They were wildly enthusiastic.

In January 1968, fifty workers drove all the way to New York in an old, unheated school bus. Others went to different cities. They asked store owners not to sell grapes. They asked shoppers not to buy them.

Everywhere the workers went, people volunteered to carry signs in front of stores: DON'T BUY GRAPES! Truck drivers, too, wanted to help. Some refused to take grapes from vineyards to stores. Others refused to load them onto ships for sending to countries across the ocean.

The next year the boycott spread into more parts of the country. Cesar was overjoyed. He believed that at last he had found a way to show the problems of all farm workers to the whole United States.

Cesar is now middle-aged. His dark skin is unlined and his hair is heavy and black. But he is tired and thin. Doing stoop labor for so many years injured his back. The injury is very painful.

A group of friends take turns caring for him. When he goes to a meeting, they help him up and down stairs. Because he is so important to them, they all want to protect him and to help him in any way they can.

In spite of struggle and hardship and pain, Cesar has not changed very much. He is still the soft-voiced, patient leader. He takes as much time to talk with a picker about his personal problems as with a newspaper reporter about the boycott. He and his family still live no better than other workers.

Cesar is happy to see the changes that have come to farm workers since he was a boy. They have better housing and wages. They have rest periods during the day, and some are paid when they are too sick to work. Their children go to school.

But he now lives for the future. He firmly believes that some day the Congress of the United

States will treat farm workers the same as all other workers in the country. He believes it will give leaders of farm-workers' unions the right to settle problems with farm owners—a right they do not yet have.

When that day comes, Cesar Chavez believes, farm workers will no longer be the forgotten Americans.

ABOUT THE AUTHOR

Even before she set out to write this biography of Cesar Chavez, Ruth Franchere was especially concerned with the plight of migratory farm workers. Her husband was on the governor's committee to examine all aspects of the lives of these workers in Oregon some years ago, and she has always remembered his stories about the poor living conditions and the exploitation of many of the migrants.

Mrs. Franchere lived in Waterloo, Iowa, until her marriage. She was graduated from the University of Iowa and then spent some years in Illinois and California. Now she makes her home in Oregon, where her husband is Dean of the Division of Arts and Letters at Portland State University. She and her husband live in a delightful lake community, just a few hours from both the mountains and the sea.

ABOUT THE ILLUSTRATOR

Earl Thollander has traveled throughout much of the world, and he is now happy to remain on his large, hilly ranch with a forest that is his own and deer grazing outside his window. There, when he is not working, he can relax by practicing forestry or playing the guitar.

Mr. Thollander studied art at the University of California. He has had some one-man shows and has had three of his books chosen as Best Books at recent exhibits of the American Institute of Graphic Arts.

42